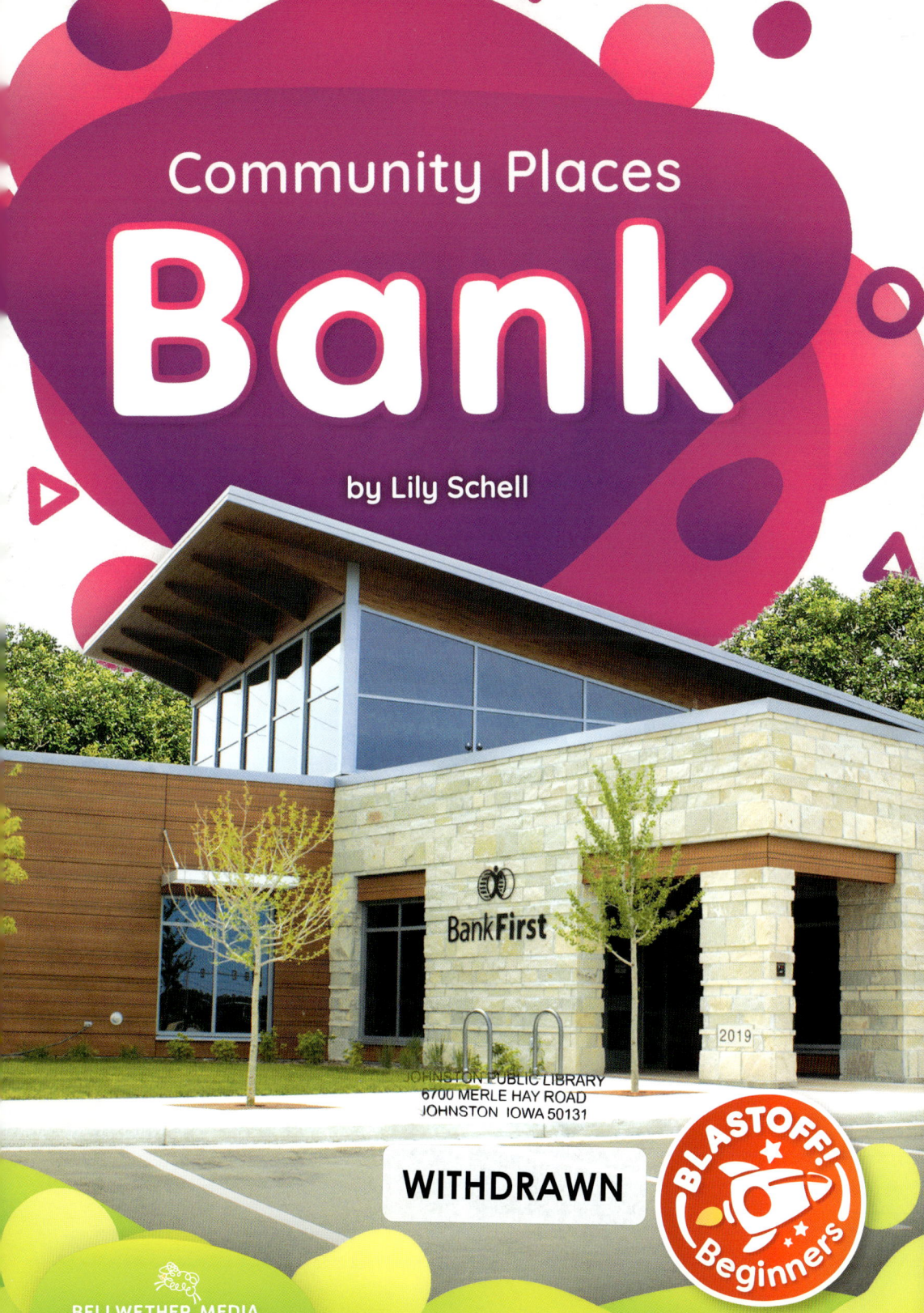

Community Places
Bank

by Lily Schell

BELLWETHER MEDIA
MINNEAPOLIS, MN

Blastoff! Beginners are developed by literacy experts and educators to meet the needs of early readers. These engaging informational texts support young children as they begin reading about their world. Through simple language and high frequency words paired with crisp, colorful photos, Blastoff! Beginners launch young readers into the universe of independent reading.

Sight Words in This Book

a	he	out	this
an	help	people	to
are	into	she	too
at	is	the	we
from	it	their	with
get	our	they	

This edition first published in 2023 by Bellwether Media, Inc.

No part of this publication may be reproduced in whole or in part without written permission of the publisher. For information regarding permission, write to Bellwether Media, Inc., Attention: Permissions Department, 6012 Blue Circle Drive, Minnetonka, MN 55343.

Library of Congress Cataloging-in-Publication Data

Names: Schell, Lily, author.
Title: Bank / Lily Schell.
Description: Minneapolis, MN : Bellwether Media, 2023. | Series: Blastoff! Beginners: Community places | Includes bibliographical references and index. | Audience: Ages 4-7 | Audience: Grades K-1
Identifiers: LCCN 2022002380 (print) | LCCN 2022002381 (ebook) | ISBN 9781644876657 (library binding) | ISBN 9781648347115 (ebook)
Subjects: LCSH: Banks and banking--Juvenile literature. | Banks and banking--Customer services--Juvenile literature.
Classification: LCC HG1609 .S24 2023 (print) | LCC HG1609 (ebook) | DDC 332.1--dc23/eng/20220119
LC record available at https://lccn.loc.gov/2022002380
LC ebook record available at https://lccn.loc.gov/2022002381

Text copyright © 2023 by Bellwether Media, Inc. BLASTOFF! BEGINNERS and associated logos are trademarks and/or registered trademarks of Bellwether Media, Inc.

Editor: Betsy Rathburn   Designer: Gabriel Hilger

Printed in the United States of America, North Mankato, MN.

Table of Contents

At the Bank!	4
What Are Banks?	6
Keeping Money Safe	10
Bank Facts	22
Glossary	23
To Learn More	24
Index	24

At the Bank!

Mom needs to get money. We are at the bank!

What Are Banks?

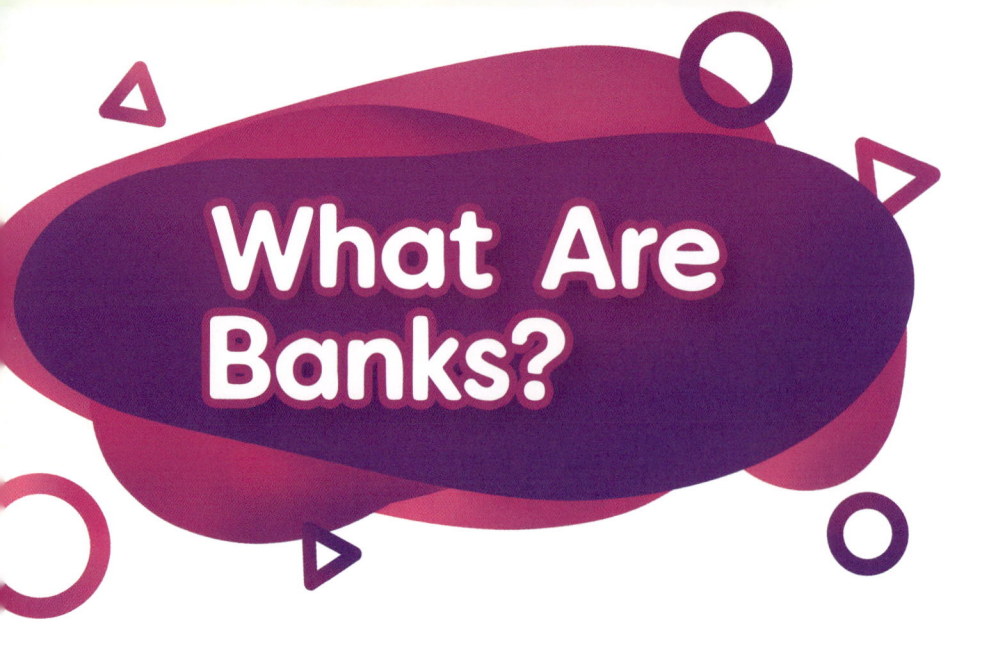

Banks are useful places. They work with money.

Banks help people save money. They lend people money, too.

Keeping Money Safe

This is an **ATM**. People get cash from it.

ATM

This is a **teller**.
He helps people
with **accounts**.

People put money into accounts. They take out money, too.

This is the **vault**.
It holds money.

This is a banker. She helps people with their money.

Banks keep our money safe!

Bank Facts

At the Bank

teller
money
banker

What Happens in a Bank?

save money

lend money

use ATM

Glossary

accounts

ways of keeping and spending money

ATM

a machine that gives people cash from their accounts

teller

a person who works with money in accounts

vault

the part of a bank where money is stored

To Learn More

ON THE WEB

FACTSURFER

Factsurfer.com gives you a safe, fun way to find more information.

1. Go to www.factsurfer.com.

2. Enter "bank" into the search box and click 🔍.

3. Select your book cover to see a list of related content.

Index

accounts, 12, 14
ATM, 10
banker, 18, 19
cash, 10
help, 8, 12, 18
lend, 8
mom, 4
money, 4, 6, 8, 9, 14, 16, 18, 20
safe, 20
save, 8
teller, 12, 13
vault, 16, 17

The images in this book are reproduced through the courtesy of: Lisa Schulz, front cover; paulaphoto, p. 3; traveler1116, p. 4; YinYang, pp. 4-5, 14-15; Bob Daemmrich/ Alamy, pp. 6-7, 23 (teller); Syda Productions, pp. 8-9, 22 (save money); leolintang, p. 10; LumineImages, pp. 10-11; TMLsPhotoG, p. 12; Hiya Images/ Corbis/ Getty Images, pp. 12-13, 20-21; kali9, p. 16; Andrew Sacks/ Getty Images, pp. 16-17; Mila Supinskaya Glashchenko, pp. 18-19; dcdebs, p. 22 (at the bank); SOUTHERNTraveler, p. 22 (lend money); Zamrznuti tonovi, p. 22 (use ATM); create jobs 51, p. 23 (accounts); PRESSLAB, p. 23 (ATM); Antonello Aringhieri, p. 23 (vault).